£2.50

D1344138

*Cover photograph*
Arthur's Stone, Dorstone, Herefordshire.
(Photograph: Leslie V. Grinsell.)

British Library Cataloguing in Publication Data:
Grinsell, L. V. (Leslie Valentine), *1907-*
Barrows in England and Wales.
-3rd ed. (Shire Archaeology; 8).
1. England. Burial places, Barrows.
I. Title.
936. 2'33
ISBN 0-7478-0052-9

Published by
SHIRE PUBLICATIONS LTD,
Cromwell House, Church Street, Princes Risborough,
Buckinghamshire HP17 9AJ, UK.

Series Editor: James Dyer.

ISBN 0 7478 0052 9.

First published in 1979.
Second edition 1984.
Third edition 1990.

Printed in Great Britain by
C. I. Thomas & Sons (Haverfordwest) Ltd,
Press Buildings, Merlins Bridge, Haverfordwest, Dyfed SA61 1XF.

# Contents

LIST OF ILLUSTRATIONS 4

1. TERMINOLOGY 5

2. HISTORY OF STUDY 7

3. NEOLITHIC PERIOD 9

4. EARLIER BRONZE AGE 30

5. LATER BRONZE AGE 47

6. IRON AGE 49

7. ROMAN PERIOD 51

8. ANGLO-SAXON AND VIKING PERIODS 53

9. MUSEUMS 57

10. FURTHER READING 60

SITE INDEX 63

4

# List of illustrations

1. Duggleby Howe, North Yorkshire *page 10*
2. Silbury Hill, Wiltshire *page 10*
3. Long Bredy bank-barrow, Dorset *page 11*
4. Belas Knap long barrow, Gloucestershire *page 13*
5. Belas Knap long barrow, Gloucestershire: plan *page 13*
6. Avening long barrow, Gloucestershire: porthole chamber *page 13*
7. Tinkinswood long barrow, Glamorgan: plan *page 14*
8. Tinkinswood long barrow, Glamorgan *page 15*
9. Wayland's Smithy, Oxfordshire: plan *page 16*
10. Wayland's Smithy, Oxfordshire: facade and entrance *page 17*
11. West Kennet long barrow, Wiltshire: plan *page 18*
12. West Kennet long barrow, Wiltshire *page 18*
13. East Kennet long barrow, Wiltshire *page 19*
14. Stoney Littleton long barrow, Avon: plan *page 20*
15. Stoney Littleton long barrow, Avon: entrance *page 21*
16. Kit's Coty, Kent *page 22*
17. Coldrum long barrow, Kent *page 22*
18. Bridestones long barrow, Congleton, Cheshire *page 23*
19. Bryn Celli Ddu, Anglesey *page 25*
20. Brane entrance-grave, Cornwall: plan *page 26*
21. Brane entrance-grave, Cornwall *page 26*
22. Five Wells barrow, Derbyshire: plan *page 28*
23. Five Wells barrow, Derbyshire *page 28*
24. Rillaton stone-lined grave, Cornwall *page 31*
25. Fernworthy stone cist, Dartmoor *page 32*
26. Winterslow bell-barrow, Wiltshire *page 34*
27. Upwey disc-barrow, Dorset *page 35*
28. Winterbourne Stoke Crossroads group, Wiltshire *page 36*
29. Winterbourne Stoke Crossroads group, Wiltshire: plan *page 37*
30. Lambourn Seven Barrows, Berkshire *page 38*
31. Lambourn Seven Barrows, Berkshire: barrow 1 *page 39*
32. Oakley Down group, Dorset *page 40-1*
33. Flat Howe, Sleights Moor, North Yorkshire *page 45*
34. Garleigh Moor stone cist, Northumberland *page 46*
35. Bryn yr Ellyllon, Clwyd: notice near site of barrow *page 47*
36. Bryn yr Ellyllon, Clwyd: the gold cape *page 48*
37. Littlethorpe group, Humberside *page 50*
38. Bartlow Hills, Essex *page 51*
39. Breach Down group, Kent *page 54*
40. Taplow barrow, Buckinghamshire *page 54*
41. Sutton Hoo group, Suffolk *page 55*

# 1
# Terminology

## Barrows and their structure

The word *barrow* means a mound of earth or stones erected over the bones of one or more human beings. The term *cairn* is used for a barrow composed entirely or mostly of stones. The terms *ring-barrow* and *ring-cairn* are used for a type of monument so far identified mainly in Scotland and Wales, with a few in the upland parts of England, comprising a circle of earth or stones enclosing a flat open area containing interments or evidence of funerary ritual. A circle of stones defining the circumference of a round barrow is called a *retaining circle*. The term *retaining kerb* is used where the stones form a continuous wall (figures 19-22). These circles or kerbs can be *inner* (if within the circumference), *outer* (if on the circumference) or *free-standing* (if well clear of it). In stoneless regions similar features were sometimes of wood.

A *chamber* (as usually in neolithic barrows) has an entrance and is sometimes subdivided by one or more *septal slabs*. A *cist* (as in many round barrows of the bronze age) is closed in. In areas where suitable stone slabs are available cists are usually lined with slabs and roofed with one or more *capstones*. A cavity to receive an interment is called a *grave* if for an unburnt burial, a *pit* or *cist* if for a burnt interment, and a *shaft* if unusually deep.

## Grouping in cemeteries

Barrow cemeteries can be classified as *linear* (figure 28), *nucleated* (figure 32) or *dispersed*, but these terms often express tendencies rather than clear-cut divisions. Linear grouping is often conditioned by the local topography (for example, Ninebarrow Down, Purbeck, Dorset).

## Methods of interment

The term *inhumation* is used for unburnt interments, and the term *cremation* for those which have been burnt. The *posture* of an inhumation was usually *contracted* in the neolithic, early bronze age and early iron age, and usually *extended* or slightly *flexed* in the pagan Saxon period. Occasionally, as with chieftain burials, those of the early bronze age were extended, as probably with the primary interment in Bush Barrow south-west of Stonehenge.

**Sequence of interments**

The *position* of an interment in a barrow can be below, on or above the original turf-line, and these three positions generally indicate their chronological sequence. Modern excavations in several round barrows on and around Salisbury Plain have revealed a central interment accompanied by others on either side and most likely contemporary. The *orientation* of an inhumation (stated head end first) indicates its placing in relation to the points of the compass; thus southeast-northwest means that the body was placed with the head at the south-east and the feet at the north-west.

The first interment in a barrow, usually below but sometimes on the ground level, is known as the *primary* interment. Contemporary interments, often assumed to be of relatives or retainers, are sometimes described as *satellite* or *subsidiary* interments. Near-contemporary interments are sometimes described as *subsequent primary*. The term *secondary* interment is generally used for interments of a later date but perhaps of descendants of the primary interment. The writer prefers the term *intrusive* interment for those of iron age, Roman or Saxon date inserted into earlier barrows.

# 2
# History of study

Apart from the activities of the treasure hunter, which have never ceased, perhaps the earliest recorded interest in barrows was during the earlier medieval period when some were opened by the pious looking for bones which they identified as those of saints and removed to monasteries to work miracles. The formal literature otherwise opens with a short tract on *Artificial Hills, Mounts or Burrows*, by Sir Thomas Browne (1658; printed 1683), followed by a more detailed study by John Aubrey in his *Monumenta Britannica* (1665-93; published 1980-2). Both these writers thought that barrows were the burial places of those killed in battle.

The first person to open barrows for information rather than loot was William Stukeley, who investigated several round barrows near Stonehenge in 1722-3 and whose attribution of the various types of long and round barrow to the several orders of the Druid priesthood forms a picturesque episode of eighteenth-century antiquarianism. Knowledge of the Anglo-Saxon barrows of Kent and elsewhere was advanced by Bryan Faussett (*Inventorium Sepulchrale*, 1856) and James Douglas (*Nenia Britannica*, 1793). The foundations of scientific examination of barrows on and around Salisbury Plain were laid by William Cunnington and Sir Richard Colt Hoare (*Ancient Wiltshire* I, 1812; II, 1819). By comparison Charles Warne's *Celtic Tumuli of Dorset* (1866) is disappointing, largely because he seldom gave the precise location of the barrows he explored. William Bateman and his son Thomas, in their exploration of barrows in Derbyshire and Staffordshire (*Ten Years' Diggings*, 1861) paid special attention to the human remains, an aspect further developed by J. B. Davis and John Thurnam (*Crania Britannica*, 1865). The latter's 'Ancient British Barrows' (*Archaeologia*, xlii and xliii, 1869-71) comprised a synthesis of all previous work.

The lighter side of early nineteenth-century barrow digging is provided by *The Barrow Diggers: a Dialogue in Imitation of the Grave Diggers in Hamlet*, by Charles Woolls (1839), and *Barrow-Digging by a Barrow Knight* (1845) by The Bard (Stephen Isaacson), both very scarce but summarised in *The Early Barrow Diggers* (1974) by Barry M. Marsden.

The intellectual climate which led to the founding of most of the county archaeological societies from the mid nineteenth century onwards stimulated barrow study in most areas occupied in later prehistoric times. During the same period the publication of the first edition of the 6 inches to the mile Ordnance Survey maps provided for the first time the cartographical precision required for the precise identification of the sites investigated and for detailed regional surveys.

The spate of barrow digging which accompanied and followed the establishment of the county archaeological societies has been reviewed for England by Barry Marsden (1974) and for Wales far more expertly by H. E. Roese (1986, 1987), who has noted that much of the digging was done by the clergy and other 'white collar' classes, often to prove or disprove their own theories. Yet out of such explorations grew the modern techniques of barrow excavation.

The broad characteristics of the long and round barrows of the northern English counties were stated in William Greenwell's *British Barrows* (1877), though without the topographical precision of the large-scale maps. This precision was better achieved by J. R. Mortimer (*Forty Years' Researches in British and Saxon Burial Mounds of East Yorkshire*, 1905). Data for those in Cornwall were provided by W. Copeland Borlase (*Naenia Cornubiae*, 1872) and with good plans by Borlase and W. C. Lukis ('Typical Specimens of Cornish barrows', *Archaeologia* xlix, 181-98, 1885).

The work of Lieutenant General Pitt-Rivers revolutionised the techniques of excavation and he applied his standards to *Wor Barrow* long barrow on Cranborne Chase and to several round barrows in the same area. On Dartmoor the recording of round barrows to a high standard was done by R. N. Worth and his son R. Hansford Worth from 1880 until 1950 and this and more recent work are the subject of a synthesis (Grinsell, 1979).

The development of modern techniques for excavating long barrows has been described by Paul Ashbee (1984) and further demonstrated by W. J. Britnell and others (1984) and Alan Saville (1983) at the *Hazleton North* long barrow on the Cotswolds. The subject of neolithic round barrows has been reviewed by Ian Kinnes (1979).

For bronze age round barrows Sir Cyril Fox (1959) showed how the data exposed by the spade can be interpreted by the brilliant use of a disciplined imagination. Since then many round barrows have been excavated to high standards by Paul Ashbee and others, for example Lawson *et al.*, 1986.

# 3
# Neolithic period

## ROUND BARROWS

Certain or probable neolithic round barrows, both chambered and unchambered, have been analysed by Ian Kinnes (1979), who has shown that on present evidence they are most frequent in east Yorkshire, with a sprinkling on the Cotswolds, in Wessex and elsewhere. They are here considered before long barrows because round cairns (in this context sometimes called rotundas) have been found enclosing cists or chambers within long barrows, notably at *Notgrove* and *Sales Lot* (Withington) on the Cotswolds and *Pen-y-Wyrlod* in Powys (Britnell 1984, 35); but opinions differ as to whether these round cairns are substantially earlier than the long barrows enclosing them or merely a structural phase in the building of the long barrow, as the writer believes.

Near the Gypsey Race between Malton and Scarborough there are two exceptionally large round barrows: *Duggleby Howe* (figure 1), 36 metres in diameter and now 6 metres high, which contained a primary skeleton and fifteen subsequent primary inhumations, contracted wherever sufficiently preserved, some with neolithic grave-goods, above which were more than fifty cremations (Kinnes *et al.*, 1983); and *Willy Howe*, which has no excavation record but could well have a comparable history. The radiocarbon date for Silbury Hill (figure 2), *c.*2500 BC, shows that, whatever its purpose, it is also neolithic. An unusual round barrow known as the *Soldiers' Grave*, north of the *Nympsfield* long barrow on the Cotswolds, contained in its centre a boat-shaped hollow lined with dry-stone walling, in which were the remains of up to 44 individuals, mostly unburnt.

'Free-standing' chambered round barrows will be discussed later in this chapter.

## LONG BARROWS (NON-MEGALITHIC)

'Earthen' long barrows are here described before chambered long barrows because *Wayland's Smithy II* (chambered) was superimposed on *Wayland's Smithy I* ('earthen') and because the radiocarbon dates so far obtained from long barrows suggest that the earliest are the earthen ones, although they flourished together for more than a millennium (*c.*3700 to 2500 BC). For these barrows the term *unchambered* is undesirable as they often

**1.** Duggleby Howe, North Yorkshire.

**2.** Silbury Hill, Wiltshire. (Photograph: L. V. Grinsell.)

contain wooden structures somewhat akin to the stone-built chambers. The term *earthen* should be understood to mean usually chalk but sometimes earthen in the strict sense (as *Therfield Heath*, Hertfordshire), and occasionally even including sarsens (as *Wayland's Smithy I*). Their distribution is necessarily in areas where suitable stone slabs are absent or rare, notably the Wessex chalk south of the Vale of Pewsey, the Chilterns and East Anglia, and the wolds of Lincolnshire and Yorkshire.

Their length varies from about 20 metres to about 125 metres (*East Heslerton*, North Yorkshire). A few longer examples are usually classed as *bank-barrows* but may have had the same function: in Dorset, *Long Bredy* (figure 3, 197 metres), *Maiden Castle* (545 metres); in Cumbria, *Lowther* (274 metres). The width of the normal long barrows is usually between one-half and one-quarter of their length. Their height (where not reduced by ploughing) varies between 1 metre and 7 metres (*Adam's Grave*, Wiltshire). In plan they tend to be either trapezoidal (the shorter ones) or rectangular (the longer ones).

The mound is usually formed of material derived from quarry-ditches, which normally occur only on the long sides and do not go round the ends, but sometimes they are inturned at the ends. On Cranborne Chase, however, they generally have a U-shaped

**3.** Long Bredy bank-barrow, Dorset. (Photograph: Professor J. K. St Joseph, Cambridge University Aerial Survey; copyright reserved.)

ditch, the opening of which can be at either end, or a causewayed ditch (*Wor Barrow*). That on *Therfield Heath* (Hertfordshire) has a continuous ditch. Occasionally there is a well marked berm or platform between the mound and the side-ditches, as *Pimperne* (Dorset) and *Winterbourne Stoke Crossroads* (figure 28).

The orientation of the mound is usually east-west, southeast-northwest, northeast-southwest, or intermediate positions, the higher and wider or 'business' end being eastward. Precise orientation was sometimes related to the axis of the hills on which they are placed or to man-made features, of which the chief are the cursuses in Dorset and Wiltshire.

The external features just described have been shown by excavation in several examples to cover elaborate timber structures, normally rectangular or trapezoidal and frequently with a facade, those so far exposed being convex or straight in Wessex but concave in Lincolnshire and Yorkshire. At the *Fussell's Lodge* long barrow (Wiltshire) on the floor level at the eastern end was a deposit of more than fifty interments, placed within an elaborate timber structure. It is thought that in some instances the bodies were first placed in a mortuary enclosure and later transferred to the long barrow. Such a mortuary enclosure was located on *Normanton Down* south of Stonehenge, but the only sign of it now is a soil-mark. The posture of the articulated skeletons is contracted. Cremations in the strict sense do not seem to exist in a primary context in earthen long barrows, but some of the bones are often partially burned from the firing of the mortuary enclosure, notably in and around Yorkshire.

A few earthen long barrows, excavated under modern conditions, have revealed no evidence of any burials; they may have been built in memory of persons drowned, killed in battle, or whose bodies could for some other reason not be recovered.

Both earthen and chambered long barrows normally had only the eastern or 'business' end used for burial, and the remainder of the mound, which may sometimes have been periodically length-ened, is believed to have performed a social function — such as to consolidate the community by uniting them to perform a common task.

## LONG BARROWS: CHAMBERED

Since the late 1960s there has been much fresh thinking on the typology of chambered long barrows. The idea that they develop-ed from the true to the false entrance type has given place to the

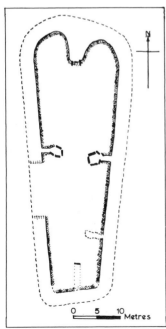

**4.** (Top) Belas Knap, Gloucestershire. (Photograph: Professor J. K. St Joseph, Cambridge University Aerial Survey: copyright reserved.)
**5.** (Left) Belas Knap long barrow, Gloucestershire: plan.
**6.** (Above) Avening long barrow, Gloucestershire: porthole chamber. (Photograph: L. V. Grinsell.)

possibility that the 'false entrance' was not a false entrance at all but a survival of the portal-dolmen, of which most examples are in the West Country. The following classification of the Cotswold-Severn group is believed to have general support at the time of writing.

**The Cotswold-Severn group**
**(a) The Belas Knap/Rodmarton type**, with 'portal-dolmen' in horned forecourt and chambers entered normally from the long sides of the mound.

*Belas Knap*, Gloucestershire (figures 4, 5), beautifully restored in 1931, has a 'portal-dolmen' structure between horns, of which the lower part of the dry-stone walling is original. The two main lateral chambers are almost opposed. The south-east chamber, of smaller stones, might be later. The south chamber is uncertain. The restored ceilings are 'crazy-paved' as the restorers of 1931 were uncertain whether they were originally flat or corbelled. The three certain chambers yielded the bones of about thirty individuals in all.

*Rodmarton* (Windmill Tump), Gloucestershire. This would be the classic example but both the lateral chambers, each with

**7.** Tinkinswood long barrow, Glamorgan: plan. (After John Ward.)

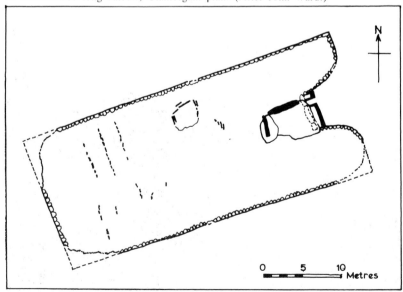

porthole entrance, are blocked to protect them from winter frosts and vandals.

*Avening*, Gloucestershire. Three burial chambers were removed from a local long barrow and re-erected in the hillslope west of the village about 1806. One of them has the porthole entrance here illustrated (figure 6). These have been re-sited a short distance away, but the porthole chamber does not seem to have been reassembled very satisfactorily.

*Ty Isaf*, Brecknock, Powys, is placed north-south with a 'portal-dolmen' between horns at the north end and has two opposed lateral chambers. The south part is occupied by an oval structure with a gallery entered from the south-east containing a pair of side-chambers, probably the whole structure being contemporary. Remains of at least 33 interments came from the chambers.

**(b) The Tinkinswood/St Lythans type**, with one chamber behind the portal.

*Tinkinswood*, Glamorgan (figures 7, 8). Excavation by John Ward in 1914 revealed more than fifty interments in the chamber.

*St Lythans*, about 1 km south-east of the last, is of similar type

**8.** Tinkinswood long barrow, Glamorgan. (Photograph: L. V. Grinsell.)

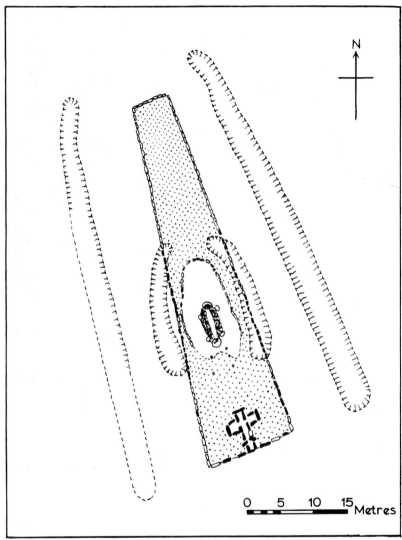

**9.** Wayland's Smithy, Oxfordshire: plan. (After R. J. C. Atkinson.)

**10.** Wayland's Smithy, Oxfordshire: facade and entrance. (Photograph: J. E. Little.)

but the mound has been much reduced in height, probably by former cultivation.

*Ty Illtud* (the hermitage of St Illtud), with its chamber set well back behind the entrance, is probably of this type. It is of special interest for having been christianised by being named from the Breton-Welsh saint and incised with numerous crosses and other symbols on the interior wall-slabs.

**(c) The Nympsfield/Stoney Littleton type**, with portal leading to a gallery with one, two or three pairs of side-chambers and usually an end-chamber.

*(i) With one pair of side-chambers*
    *Nympsfield*, now in a public recreation area and partly restored.
    *Wayland's Smithy* (figures 9, 10), a classic example excavated by R. J. C. Atkinson and now partly restored. It contained the remains of eight skeletons.

*(ii) With two pairs of side-chambers*
    *Hetty Pegler's Tump*, Uley, Gloucestershire. The two northern

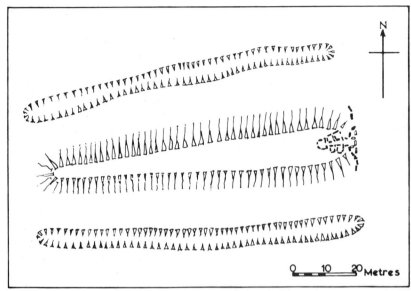

**11.** West Kennet long barrow, Wiltshire: plan. (After S. Piggott.)

**12.** West Kennet long barrow, Wiltshire. (Photograph: Aerofilms Limited.)

chambers are blocked in and were probably destroyed in 1821. At least fifteen skeletons were found in it in 1821 and 1854.

*Parc Cwm*, Gower: unusual in having no end-chamber. Excavation by R. J. C. Atkinson in 1960-1 revealed remains of at least 24 individuals. It has been partly restored.

*West Kennet*, Wiltshire (figures 11-12): perhaps the most impressive chambered long barrow in England. Excavation by Piggott in 1955-6 revealed remains of at least 46 individuals. The lower levels of the filling of the interior have been interpreted as evidence of continued usage for ritual perhaps connected with ancestor worship. In the late neolithic the interior was finally filled and the entrance blocked. The site has been partly restored.

### (iii) With three pairs of side-chambers

*Stoney Littleton*, Avon (figures 14, 15). Features of interest include an ammonite cast on the west door jamb, the stump of a closing slab at the entrance and a septal slab before the central pair of side-chambers. Perfunctory exploration by John Skinner in 1816-17 revealed the bones of several individuals.

**13.** East Kennet long barrow, Wiltshire. (Photograph: L. V. Grinsell.)

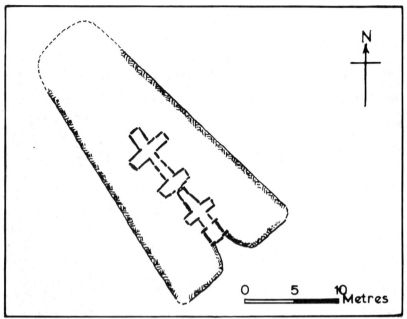

**14.** Stoney Littleton long barrow, Avon: plan.

In the Cotswold-Severn area there is one site difficult to classify: *Heston Brake* (Gwent), a long cairn placed east-west with a single very long chamber extending from the eastern end.

## The Medway group

The affinities of this group are uncertain. The finding of a polished flint axe of Scandinavian or Dutch type in the core of *Julliberrie's Grave* long barrow near Chilham suggests a possible link with Denmark or the Netherlands but this is no more than a guess.

*Kit's Coty* (figure 16) originally comprised a long mound now almost levelled by cultivation, at the south-east end of which is what appears to be a typical portal-dolmen. There are, however, no indications of any lateral chambers such as this interpretation would imply. *Lower Kit's Coty* may be the remains of a burial chamber. The *Addington* long barrow is placed northeast-south-west and has possible chambering at the north-east end and the remains of a sarsen retaining wall along both sides. It is cut by a road. *Coldrum* (figure 17) is the best preserved of the group. It comprises a rectangular mound 27 by 18 metres with all four sides

**15.** Stoney Littleton long barrow, Avon: the entrance showing the ammonite cast in the west door jamb. (Photograph: L. V. Grinsell.)

16. Kit's Coty, Kent. (Photograph: James Dyer.)
17. Coldrum long barrow, Kent. (Photograph: L. V. Grinsell.)

defined by a retaining wall of sarsens. At the east end is a rectangular chamber which contained about 22 human skeletons. *The Chestnuts* was excavated in 1957 by John Alexander, who uncovered a rectangular burial chamber in which were the burnt bones of at least nine individuals; unburnt bones may have been destroyed by the acid soil. Grave-goods comprised neolithic and early bronze age pottery and leaf-shaped and barbed-and-tanged

**18.** Bridestones long barrow, Congleton, Cheshire. (Photograph: L. V. Grinsell.)

flint arrowheads. The chamber was at the eastern end of a 'short' long barrow.

There is a site-guide, *The Medway Megaliths*, by Brian Philp and Mike Dutto (Kent Archaeological Trust, second edition 1985).

### Other sites

This is a selection of the many sites in other regions.

*Lanyon* (west Cornwall), beside the road from Penzance to Morvah, is a burial chamber with the capstone inaccurately replaced *c*.1824, at the north end of a long mound now barely visible.

*Corringdon Ball* (south Dartmoor) is 40 by 20 metres and has remains of chambering at its south-southeast end.

The *Grey Mare and Her Colts* (south Dorset) has a terminal chamber behind the remains of a crescentic forecourt at the east end of a long mound.

*The Bridestones*, Congleton (Cheshire) (figure 18), is the remains of a long barrow placed east-west with a crescentic forecourt behind which is a rectangular chamber divided transversely by a porthole slab, of which the lower part remains. The chamber had been blocked by a closing slab.

## ROUND BARROWS (CHAMBERED)

### The Anglesey group

*Barclodiad y Gawres* (the Giantess's Apronful) is a round cairn with turf core, enclosing cruciform chambering entered from a passage to the north-west. Excavation by Powell and Daniel brought to light cremations of two individuals in the west chamber. Five of the wall-slabs of the passage and chambers are decorated with motifs including spirals, lozenges, zigzags and chevrons. The present roofing is modern.

*Bryn Celli Ddu* (the Hill of the Dark Grove) (figure 19), whose plan shows two structural phases, was a circular cairn from which a passage leads from the north-east to a polygonal chamber containing a free-standing monolith. Behind this chamber and in the centre of the mound was a meander-decorated slab (cast on site; original in the National Museum of Wales) beside a pit. The mound has been restored smaller than the original to expose the outermost of four concentric circles of stones.

*Bryn yr Hen Bobl* (the Hill of the Old People) is a kidney-shaped cairn with chamber entered from the north, which contain-

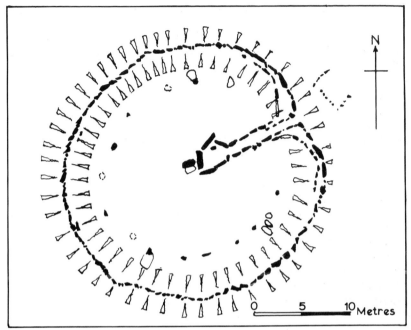

**19.** Bryn Celli Ddu, Anglesey: plan. (After W. J. Hemp.)

ed the remains of more than twenty individuals. To the south extends a long narrow projection, the purpose of which is unknown.

*Plas Newydd*, in parkland south-west of the Menai bridge, is an impressive bipartite burial chamber but it has lost its covering mound and has no excavation record.

### The Gower group
*Arthur's Stone* on Cefn Bryn, a huge boulder forming the capstone of a bipartite burial chamber by underpinning with smaller stones, is believed to stand on the remains of a round cairn.

The two *Sweyne's Howes* on the east slope of Rhossili Down each comprise a burial chamber within a mound of nearly circular form.

### The Scilly/Penwith entrance-graves
This group, represented by at least fifty sites in the Scilly

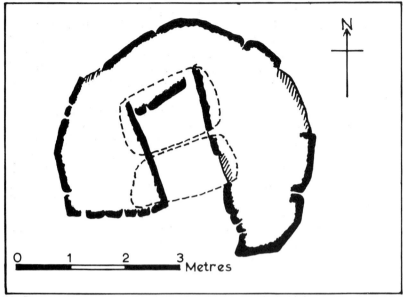

**20.** Brane entrance-grave, Cornwall: plan. (After W. C. Lukis.)

**21.** Brane entrance-grave, Cornwall. (Photograph: L. V. Grinsell.)

Islands and four in west Cornwall, comprises circular cairns with a retaining kerb and usually a parallel-sided chamber entered from the east or south-east. As the entrance leads straight into the chamber they are usually called entrance-graves. Their diameter averages between 4 and 12 metres and their height up to 3 metres. In Scilly they are sometimes built around a natural outcrop.

Among the best known in Scilly is *Bant's Carn* (St Mary's), an oval cairn about 9 by 6 metres, with a chamber entered from the east, covered by four capstones (the outermost and its jamb were replaced in 1970). This cairn is defined by a good retaining kerb, and well outside this is an outer kerb giving a total overall diameter of about 13 metres, and a walled passage connects this outer kerb with the entrance to the chamber. Four piles of cremated bones were found at the back of the chamber, and in the passage were potsherds, probably bronze age. The best example in the Penwith area is *Brane* (figures 20, 21), but there is no record of its excavation.

### The Derbyshire Dales

The tombs in this group form a fairly compact assemblage. Excavation has shown that they have mostly yielded communal inhumations, the skulls long-headed, of both sexes and all ages. Among the best examples are:

*Five Wells*, Taddington (figures 22, 23) is on a hilltop about 425 metres above sea level. The cairn is roughly circular and about 25 metres in diameter and encloses two chambers placed back to back on a northeast-southwest axis, that at the north-east being the better preserved. Both chambers were explored by Bateman in 1846, when the remains of at least twelve inhumations were found in the chambers. Of two cists, perhaps secondary, one contained an inhumation and the other an inhumation and a cremation.

*Minninglow* is the largest in the group. The mound is about 37 metres north-south and 43 metres west-east, and rather more than 3 metres high. Chamber I, placed centrally, still has its capstone, and there is an uncleared passage extending east. Chamber II, south of centre, likewise retains its capstone, and there is a passage extending south, with a capstone remaining. Two other chambers, west and south-west of centre, are now without capstones. Bateman's excavation of 1851 did not reveal any original interments but the cairn had been robbed from Roman times onwards.

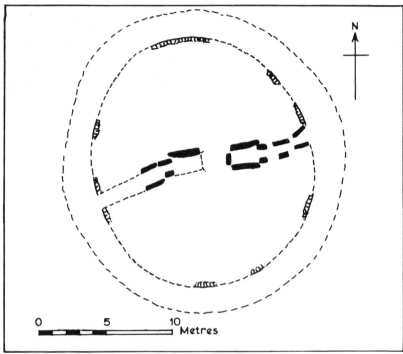

**22.** Five Wells barrow, Derbyshire: plan. (After John Ward.)

**23.** Five Wells barrow, Derbyshire. (Photograph: L. V. Grinsell.)

*Green Low*, Aldwark, is about 17 metres in diameter. Slightly south of centre is a chamber entered from the south, the capstone missing. It is separated from its passage by two septal slabs. Excavations in 1964 brought to light a disarticulated human skeleton in the mound east of the chamber and some neolithic and beaker sherds, and there was a straight entrance facade of slabs.

# 4
# Earlier bronze age

Apart from some flat graves which are outside the scope of this book, the funerary monuments of the earlier bronze age comprise round barrows and cairns. These normally cover individual interments but frequently have subsidiary or later interments added, suggesting in some instances family sepulchres extending over several generations. The richer grave-groups suggest a degree of social ranking not apparent in the neolithic.

The number of surviving round barrows of this period in England and Wales probably approaches forty thousand and only the main groups and most important examples are here described.

## THE SOUTH-WEST

### Bodmin Moor and surroundings

Of some two thousand round barrows in Cornwall, only a few notable examples are here discussed. The *Pelynt* group west of Looe is a group of about ten barrows, one of which is thought to have yielded a bronze sword-hilt of Aegean type. From there the B3359 goes north to meet the A390 at *Taphouse*, with its fine linear cemetery of barrows. About 7 km north of Liskeard, just south of the Cheesewring, is the famous *Rillaton* barrow, in the east margin of which is the stone-lined grave (figure 24) which yielded a gold cup, grooved bronze dagger and other objects with an extended male(?) skeleton in 1818. Beside a byroad just west of the Crowdy reservoir and east of Camelford is the *Advent* triple barrow, one of the only four triple barrows known — the others being at *Crooksbury* (Surrey), on *Amesbury Down* (Wiltshire) and among the *Five Knolls*, Dunstable (Bedfordshire). At *Carland Cross*, near the junction of the A30 and the A3076, is the *Carland* group, which includes a fine bell-barrow 3 metres high. Perhaps the largest round barrow in Cornwall is *Veryan Beacon* above Gerrans Bay, said to be the burial place of Gerennius, a Cornish saint and king.

### Dartmoor

Of some 650 round barrows (nearly all cairns), at least 130 of the smaller ones, mostly near rivers and streams, have a central stone cist exposed. These cists are mostly large enough to have contained a contracted interment but unburnt bones do not

**24.** Rillaton stone-lined grave, Cornwall. (Photograph: L. V. Grinsell.)

survive in the acid soil of Dartmoor. Four of these cists have yielded beakers and another three have contained other grave-goods normally found with inhumations. About six others have yielded cremations assumed to date from the early bronze age. Of some 580 small cairns about 130 have retaining circles or kerbs and at least 57 have a stone row extending from the cairn downhill, usually following the line of minimum slope. Dartmoor is the classic area for small cairns with retaining circles and stone rows. Many of them, however, are difficult to find unless one has a large-scale map, a compass and plenty of time.

Apart from the fine cist north of *Fernworthy* reservoir (figure 25) and one or two other notable sites, the more interesting cairns are on the low moor south of the road between Tavistock and Moretonhampstead. The largest group of cisted cairns is around the Plym valley between Ditsworthy Warren and Plym Steps but this involves quite a long walk. A more accessible group is on *Lakehead Hill* in Bellever Forest, where the Forestry Commission has made clearances around the cairns. The best known site here, a cairn with 'above ground' cist and retaining circle and stone row at SX 645776, is a conjectural restoration of the late nineteenth century, probably by Sabine Baring-Gould.

**25.** Fernworthy stone cist, Dartmoor. (Photograph: L. V. Grinsell.)

Among the largest Dartmoor cairns are the *Three Barrows* although they have been badly plundered. The group on *Hamel Down* includes *Two Barrows*, the northern of which yielded in 1877 a cremation with a grooved bronze dagger which had a gold pointillé-decorated amber pommel, destroyed in the blitz on Plymouth in 1941.

**South-east Devon: the Broad Down area**
An extensive scatter of ninety to a hundred round barrows on *Broad Down*, *Farway* and *Gittisham Hill*, between Sidmouth and Honiton, owes its preservation to the infertility of the land for agriculture. They include no clearly defined rare types, but among several carelessly dug by Richard Kirwan between 1867 and 1872 were two in which he found handled shale cups, one

with a grooved bronze dagger, both finds belonging to Wessex II.

### Exmoor

On the ridgeway forming the county boundary between Devon and Somerset are three barrow groups and other barrows nearby. *Setta Barrow*, a large cairn with a surrounding ditch, has a retaining kerb of slabs forced outwards by the cairn material. The cairn to the north also has traces of a retaining circle, and that 110 metres to the south has a retaining circle and a row of about three stones surviving. The *Five Barrows* is a group of nine including a well formed bell-barrow. There are four barrows in the group known as *Two Barrows* to the south-east. The linear group known as *Chapman Barrows* is remarkable for the large size of the eleven barrows in the group.

### Mendip and surroundings

Among the best linear barrow groups are the *Priddy Nine Barrows* (ST 539515) and the *Ashen Hill barrows* (ST 539521), whose names are mistakenly transposed on some Ordnance Survey maps. The Ashen Hill barrows were explored in 1815 by John Skinner, who found in them primary cremations, one with a grape-cup and part of a bronze knife-dagger. These and other barrow groups in the area may well have been sited to be in the vicinity of the *Priddy Circles*, presumed to have been ceremonial sites. At *Beacon Batch*, south-east of Burrington Combe, is a good nucleated group including a probable bell-barrow. A foot-carved cist-slab from a round barrow at *Pool Farm*, north of the *Priddy Circles*, is in the City of Bristol Museum and Art Gallery.

South of Mendip proper, in *Old Down Field*, Cranmore, just north of the disused railway line, is a group of three barrows, two being bell-barrows, each with outer bank. One was opened in 1869 and shown to contain a primary(?) cremation with grooved ogival bronze dagger.

## WESSEX

There are more than four thousand round barrows in Wessex (Wiltshire, Dorset, Hampshire and Berkshire) likely to date between the end of the Beaker phase and the Deverel-Rimbury phase which followed the 'Wessex' culture. Of these, more than five hundred are of types distinctive of that culture: about 250 bell-barrows, 160 disc-barrows, over 60 saucer-barrows and over 50 pond-barrows.

The *bell-barrow*, averaging 35-50 metres in diameter and up to 5 metres high, has a berm or platform between the mound and surrounding ditch, and occasionally an outer bank. It usually covered a primary adult male interment, occasionally by inhumation but generally cremated, with warrior equipment including a grooved bronze dagger.

The *disc-barrow* averages 35-60 metres in diameter and up to 2 metres in the height of the central mound or tump placed on a wide platform encircled by a ditch and outer bank. Sometimes additional mounds were placed between the central mound and the ditch. The central mound usually covered a cremated interment assumed to be of a female as it was generally accompanied by beads from a necklace and other items of female adornment. The sex of those interred in the secondary mounds may vary. In Dorset there is a variant 'Dorset disc-barrow', usually smaller and with a ditch on either side of the bank, or both.

The *saucer-barrow*, usually little more than half the diameter of the disc-barrow, comprises a low mound occupying the whole of the circular area defined by the ditch and outer bank. Excavation records do not indicate anything distinctive concerning those interred in them.

**26.** Winterslow bell-barrow, Wiltshire. (Photograph: L. V. Grinsell.)

**27.** Upwey disc-barrow, Dorset. (Photograph: J. K. St Joseph, Cambridge University Aerial Survey; copyright reserved.)

The *pond-barrow* comprises a circular depression surrounded by an outer bank. Its purpose is uncertain but its frequent association with barrow groups suggests that, if not itself sepulchral, it was connected with funerary ritual.

Round barrows of exceptional type include very large bell-barrows with wide berm, as at *Knowlton* and *Winterslow* (figure 26), and an enormous disc-shaped barrow with very large central mound at *Upwey* (figure 27). These are generally assumed to be of 'Wessex' culture but they have no excavation record.

The *bowl-barrow*, usually with encircling ditch, is the normal type and accounts for the remainder of some 3500 sites.

This variety in types of round barrow combines with the frequent richness of the grave-goods to emphasise that there was a ranked society wherever the 'Wessex' culture penetrated.

The most accessible groups including these types will now be described.

### Salisbury Plain

The main barrow groups around Stonehenge are now covered by waymarked archaeological trails.

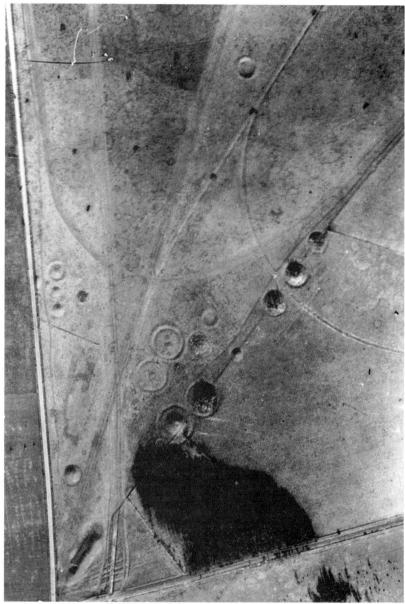

**28.** Winterbourne Stoke Crossroads group, Wiltshire. (Photograph courtesy of Air Photography Unit, RCHM National Monuments Record.)

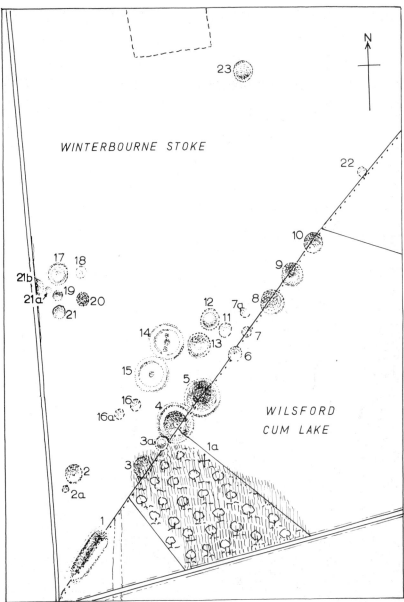

**29.** Winterbourne Stoke Crossroads group, Wiltshire.

The *Winterbourne Stoke Crossroads* group (figures 28, 29) includes every type of round barrow listed and many are aligned on a long barrow. On the plan (figure 29) 4 and 5 are bell-barrows and the latter yielded a jar of Breton type and two bronze daggers of Armorican type with a skeleton probably of an adult male. 14 and 15 are disc-barrows; 17 and 18 are saucer-barrows; and 3a and 12 are pond-barrows, 3a overlapping 4. The rest are bowl-barrows.

The *Normanton* group, unfortunately deteriorating from the use of the land for agriculture, contains examples of exceptional interest, including *Bush Barrow*, which produced one of the richest grave-groups yet known, of a man with the probable remains of a helmet above the head, bronze daggers of Armorican type, a mace-head of a rare fossil from the Teignmouth area, cylindrical bone mounts similar to those from Grave Iota of Grave Circle B at Mycenae, a lozenge-shaped breast ornament and a gold belt-hook. The group includes a twin bell-barrow, four single bell-barrows, seven disc-barrows, a saucer-barrow and

**30.** Lambourn Seven Barrows, Berkshire. (Photograph: G. W. G. Allen; copyright Ashmolean Museum, Oxford.)

about twenty bowl-barrows. There are also two small long barrows.

For other barrow groups around Stonehenge see Grinsell (1978).

## The Berkshire Downs

The *Lambourn Seven Barrows* (figures 30, 31) originally comprised about 35 sites, excluding a few outliers. The main group includes two bell-barrows, two disc-barrows, two probable saucer-barrows and two twin barrows. The rest are bowl-barrows, mostly with their encircling ditches still visible. To the north-west is a ploughed-down long barrow. Barrow 1 (figure 31), opened by Edwin Martin Atkins in the 1850s, contained a primary cremation, four secondary deposits and 112 later bronze age cremations (58 in urns), probably all in the south-western sector.

## Cranborne Chase

The *Oakley Down* group (figure 32) is notable for its disc-barrows, of which there are six, two (one an oval twin) being cut by the Ackling Dyke Roman road. The southernmost disc-barrow contained a cremation in an urn with eleven perforations round

**31.** Lambourn Seven Barrows, Berkshire: barrow 1. (Photograph: L. V. Grinsell.)

**32.** (Overleaf) Oakley Down group, Dorset. (Photograph: John White, West Air Photography.)

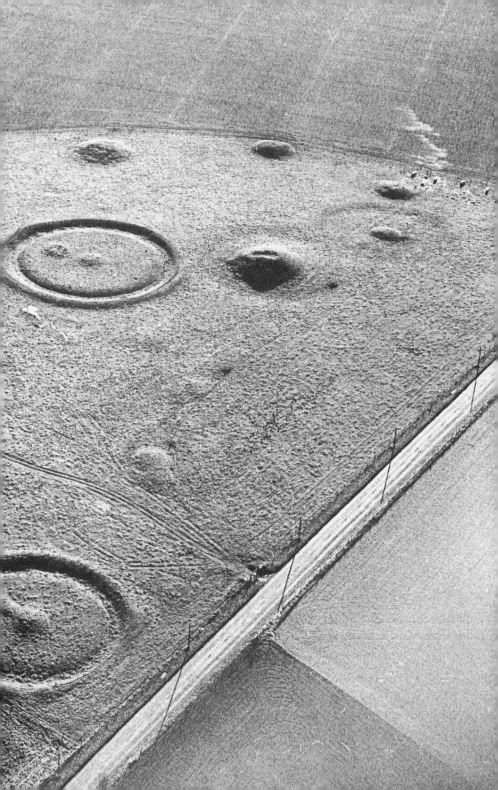

the rim for attaching a cloth cover, remains of which were found. This barrow and the bell-barrow next to it had their peripheral features reduced by cultivation, probably in Roman times, but can still be seen if looked for. The other disc-barrows have eccentrically placed tumps as well as the central tump.

### South Dorset

Along the ridgeway between the bank-barrows at *Long Bredy* and *Culliford Tree*, a distance of about 14 km, there is a vast linear cemetery of more than three hundred round barrows of all types, which led Stukeley to observe: 'for sight of barrows, I believe not to be equalled in the world' (*It. Curios.*, 1776, 163). The most accessible examples are beside the ridgeway between the Hardy Monument and Culliford Tree. The *Clandon Barrow*, north of the ridgeway and west of Maiden Castle, contained a rich grave-group which included a quadrangular gold plate, jet mace-head with gold discs and an amber cup.

Further east, on the Purbeck Hills, the group known as *Nine Barrows* comprises seventeen sites in all.

### West Sussex

From the standpoint of the distribution of round barrows of 'Wessex' types, the downland west of the Arun can be considered as part of Wessex. *The Devil's Jumps* on Treyford Hill north of Chichester are five (originally six) enormous bell-barrows, and the *Devil's Humps* (or the *Kings' Graves*) on Bow Hill includes two bell-barrows of similar size. Mid nineteenth-century ex-plorations revealed primary(?) cremations in two of each group. On the south-west spur of *Bow Hill* is a twin bell-barrow.

## WALES

### North Wales

The *Brenig Archaeological Trail* includes various types of cairn which were excavated in the early 1970s. Their restoration includes the stake circles which originally enclosed them.

### South Wales

The three cairns within *Foel Trigarn* hillfort, east of Carn Meini (the source of the Stonehenge bluestones), are probably the largest in Dyfed. On the Gower peninsula, among those along the ridge of *Rhossili Down* is an example with good retaining circle north of the Beacon. There are at least ten well defined cairns along the ridge of *Llanmadoc Hill*, on the north slope of which, beside the track, there is an example with an exposed stone cist. The thirty or more cairns along the *Cefn Bryn* (the hilly ridge) are mostly difficult to find, an exception, west of Arthur's Stone, being the *Great Carn*, stripped of its vegetation cover about 1980 to reveal its cairn structure. Down the slope to the north are two ring-cairns which were investigated at the same time. Each had an entrance which had been blocked presumably after it had served its purpose, which may have been for funerary or other ritual rather than for burial.

The group of about fifteen cairns on *Gelligaer Common* includes *Carn Bugail* (the shepherd's cairn), which may have contained three stone cists, the central of which is exposed, and has traces of a retaining kerb. Three other cairns in the group have exposed stone cists and there are several sites which appear to be ring-cairns.

A site of special interest is *Crug yr Afan* off the Rhondda valley: a 'Wessex' bell-barrow, overall diameter 30 metres and height 90 cm. Excavation in 1902 revealed a central(?) cist in which was a cremation with a grooved ogival bronze dagger.

## EAST ANGLIA

### The Icknield Way
Within a short distance of the Icknield Way, as it proceeds north-eastwards by the Chilterns into East Anglia, there are numerous barrows, including 'Wessex' types. Among the more notable are those on Dunstable Downs known as the *Five Knolls*, actually seven in all, which include a triple bell-barrow and two pond-barrows. Continuing north-eastwards, the Icknield Way passes north of the *Therfield Heath* group of ten round barrows and a long barrow.

### Breckland
On entering Breckland we come to a group south-east of Thetford called the *Seven Hills*, which includes a bell-barrow and possible disc-barrows damaged by the military during both world wars. To the north there are good groups near the Peddars Way, a Roman road possibly following a prehistoric trackway. South-west of *Little Cressingham* are the remains of a group of seven, in one of which was found a crouched male burial with grooved bronze dagger, incised rectangular gold plate and other objects. About 5 km east of the Peddars Way is the *Weasenham Lyngs*

group, which included rare types damaged by cultivation since the Second World War. To the north is a scattered group of barrows between *Anmer* and *Harpley Common*. To the north-east, on *Bircham Common*, is a group which includes bell-barrows.

## THE DERBYSHIRE DALES

Many of the round barrows in this area are still in pasture and in fair condition. *Gib Hill*, south-west of Arbor Low stone circle, is thought to be a bronze age round barrow superimposed on a neolithic barrow. The stone cist found in it by Thomas Bateman, who removed it to his garden at Lomberdale House, was replaced in its original site in 1940. The barrow is about 27 metres in diameter and 4.5 metres high, and among the largest in the area. Behind the Congregational church at Middleton-by-Youlgreave is the tomb of the barrow digger Thomas Bateman, crowned by a model of a bronze age collared urn.

The dispersed group of more than seventy cairns on *Stanton Moor*, although not very spectacular, is noted for the excavations made in many of them by J. C. and J. P. Heathcote, who restored some of them. Among the most interesting is T2, 360 metres east of the Cork Stone. A central cist contained burnt bones and parts of an urn; it had two capstones, on one of which were disturbed bones and a food vessel. The cairn has inner and outer retaining circles, partly restored. Several of the other cairns have retaining circles or kerbs.

## THE NORTHERN GROUPS

### Thornborough and Hutton Moors

Around the henge monuments on these moors (now mostly in cultivation) were until recently nearly thirty round barrows, some of considerable size and a few of which still remain. The *Centre Hill* barrow, south-east of the central Thornborough henge, was opened in 1864 by W. C. Lukis, who found in it an extended(?) inhumation with a food vessel in a dug-out coffin.

### Danby Moors

Among the more notable of the round barrows on Danby Moors is *Loose Howe*, a cairn 18 metres in diameter and 2 metres high, excavated by the Elgees in 1937. The primary burial was of an extended skeleton (inferred), probably clad in a linen garment and with a flat bronze dagger, in a dug-out coffin with its cover.

Either the coffin or its lid, or both, may or may not have originally been canoes. Above this was a secondary cremation with an urn in fragments, a grooved bronze dagger (Wessex II), a stone battle-axe, a bronze trefoil-headed pin and parts of a 'pigmy' vessel. *Flat Howe*, on Sleights Moor (figure 33), is a fine cairn with a retaining kerb.

On *Danby Rigg*, north of the Double Dykes, are four large cairns and about eight hundred very small ones of uncertain origin.

**The Northumbrian Moors**

A characteristic of many of the Northumbrian cairns is that they often contain one or more exposed stone cists. That on *Garleigh Moor* (figure 34), south-east of Rothbury, contains one; a cairn among the group on *Hepburn Moor* south of Chillingham contained two, of which one can still be seen; one of the capstones had been dressed to shape and covered a skeleton with a beaker. At *Blawearie*, north-east of Old Bewick Camps, Greenwell excavated a small cairn in which were four cists, of

**33.** Flat Howe, Sleights Moor, North Yorkshire. (Photograph: L. V. Grinsell.)

**34.** Garleigh Moor stone cist, Northumberland. (Photograph: L. V. Grinsell.)

which one was placed centrally to the retaining circle. The group known as *Five Barrows*, above Holystone west of the river Coquet, comprises numerous small cairns as well as the larger ones, two of which were explored by Greenwell, who found cremations in them, one with a food vessel.

# 5
# Later bronze age

The custom of primary interment in barrows declined rapidly after the earlier bronze age but continued chiefly in southern England and especially southern Wessex, where nearly a hundred such barrows are known. These have yielded primary cremations in urns of bucket, barrel or globular forms known as Deverel-Rimbury urns from their type sites in Dorset, the *Deverel Barrow* and the *Rimbury* cemetery. These barrows average 12 metres in diameter and under 1 metre high, being much smaller than those of the earlier bronze age, and they lack the structural refinements of the earlier round barrows. It is now believed that the Deverel-Rimbury phase began well before the end of Wessex II.

The primary interment in the *Deverel Barrow*, opened in 1825, may have been a cremation beneath an inverted collared urn of the earlier bronze age, but this was found well west of centre and the barrow may have been enlarged on its eastern side to receive the Deverel-Rimbury cremations, of which there were more than twenty. The barrow was 16.5 metres in diameter and is said to have been 3.6 metres high — perhaps an exaggeration. Two of

**35.** Bryn yr Ellyllon, Clwyd: notice near the site of the barrow. (Photograph: M. Bevan Evans.)

**36.** Bryn yr Ellyllon, Clwyd: the gold cape. (Copyright: British Museum.)

the large stones of the cairn are incised W.A.M., the initials of the excavator W. A. Miles. There are many other instances of secondary cremations in Deverel-Rimbury urns in earlier barrows.

The gold cape found with an inhumation in *Bryn yr Ellyllon* (the Hill of the Spectre), Mold (figures 35, 36), has no known parallels and might be either contemporary with Wessex II or later bronze age.

# 6
# Iron age

The only known pre-Roman iron age peoples of England and Wales whose funerary customs included barrow burial were the inhabitants of Yorkshire and Humberside. Their barrows tend to occur closely spaced in nucleated groups of up to five hundred. They are occasionally circular with a ditch around their circumference, but most of them are mounds within square ditches which supplied the material for the bulk of the mound. The mounds are usually between 3 and 12 metres across and up to 1 metre high, their overall size including ditch being up to 15 metres. Because of their small size most of the groups have been either reduced or eliminated by cultivation, sometimes only to be revealed once more by aerial photography (the *Littlethorpe* group, figure 37).

Their distribution near the Yorkshire and Humberside coast implies a relationship with the La Tène cultures of north-eastern France, where similar barrows occur. The English groups are described as of the Arras culture from a group of more than a hundred mounds at *Arras* near Market Weighton, many of which have been excavated. The more prestigious burials are cart-burials with horse harness. The vehicle was sometimes dismantled before being placed in the grave. Other burials usually contain contracted inhumations, with grave-goods limited to pots, bracelets and other objects of adornment, and pig bones.

The best preserved group, at *Garton Slack*, is not suitable for visiting as it is usually covered with brambles and nettles and adjoins a plant for processing the carcasses of animals. The next best groups are south-east of *Scorborough* (about 120 mounds) and the *Danes' Hills* on Skipwith Common.

Occasionally these square-ditched barrows are found in southern England, for example at *Handley* in Dorset, where one was shown by excavation to be iron age.

A barrow of outstanding importance but of entirely different type is the *Lexden Barrow* west of Colchester, now in the gardens of 30 and 36 Fitzwalter Road. It is 24 metres in diameter and was formerly at least 2.8 metres high, and it is ditched. Excavation in 1924 revealed a large central cavity containing the primary cremation of a male adult with gold tissue, probably from a garment, and numerous articles of bronze (chain-mail, table, folding stool, pedestal, statuette of Cupid, figurines of bull, boar and the head of a griffin). There were sherds of amphorae

**37.** Littlethorpe group, Humberside. (Photograph: D. N. Riley PhD, DFC, FSA.)

representing about eighteen vessels. These sherds, with a small silver bust of Augustus cast from a coin struck soon after 17 BC, date the deposit to *c*.15 BC or slightly later. The barrow could therefore be considered either iron age or Roman republican (Foster, 1986).

# 7
# Roman period

The custom of barrow burial in Roman times is thought to have been introduced into England from Belgium, where at least 350 Roman barrows are known.

The available evidence suggests that Roman barrows are not very numerous compared with those of the bronze age. The better known ones are large, steep and conical, for example the *Bartlow Hills* (figure 38), the largest of which is 44 metres in diameter and 13.7 metres high. Small Roman barrows are also known, both on their own, as *Knob's Crook* (Dorset) and on *Overton Hill* in Wiltshire (Fowler, 1965), and in groups, as at the appropriately named *Petty Knowes* near Rochester (Northumberland), where a group of eighty to a hundred examples averages 2-7 metres in diameter and up to 50 cm in height (Charlton *et al.*, 1984). In one instance (the *Six Hills*, Stevenage) they are aligned beside a Roman road; in others they are near a Roman villa (*Eastlow Hill*, Suffolk) or other Roman settlement (*Thornborough*, Buckinghamshire). The rite of the primary interment

**38.** Bartlow Hills, Essex. (Sketch by G. N. Maynard, 1834-1904. Copyright: Ipswich Museum Committee.)

was normally cremation, which implies a date not later than about AD 220, after which inhumation became the rule.

The only Roman barrow in England with an accessible interior is the *Mersea Mount* in Essex; when it was excavated in 1912 a concrete tunnel was made into it to enable the tiled burial chamber to be inspected. Among the more impressive examples elsewhere are the *Dane John Mound* in Dane John gardens, Canterbury, and two examples at *Thornborough*, Buckinghamshire, one 4.9 metres high and the other only slightly less.

# 8
# Anglo-Saxon and Viking periods

## Pagan Saxon barrows

The only royal and princely barrow cemetery so far known in England is at *Sutton Hoo*, Suffolk (figure 41), where the famous ship barrow is among a group of about seventeen barrows, all much larger than those of the pagan Saxon rank and file. The richness of the grave furniture combined with the absence of any trace of a human body leads to the belief that the deceased may have received Christian burial elsewhere and the balance of evidence suggests a memorial to Raedwald (died AD 625-6). The site has generated an extensive literature, but the visitor should be content with the pamphlet *Sutton Hoo* (1987) by M. O. H. Carver, available at the site.

Elsewhere, isolated large barrows of princely character average 15-20 metres in diameter and 1-4.5 metres in height. They include the *Taplow* barrow, Buckinghamshire, (figure 40), which contained the unburnt remains of an adult male (presumably Taeppa) with grave-goods including two shields, a sword, a Coptic bronze bowl, a gold buckle set with garnets, a small lyre and several glass drinking horns. The *Asthall* barrow (Oxfordshire) contained the cremated bones probably of a man, with remains of a bronze bowl, gaming pieces and one or more drinking horns and other objects. About 4.8 km south-east of Asthall is a large barrow, probably Saxon, from which Lew (= *Hlaew*) got its name. On the Ridgeway south-east of Wantage is *Scutchamer Knob* (*Cwicelmes hlaew* in the Anglo-Saxon Chronicle), which was excavated in 1934 with inconclusive results but has from the documentary evidence a strong claim to a pagan Saxon date. In the Peak District, the *Benty Grange* barrow yielded traces of an inhumation with a helmet of iron and horn crowned with a bronze boar. All these sites probably date from the first half of the seventh century AD.

Groups of small round barrows, which the writer prefers to call grave-mounds, were formerly common on the chalk downs of Kent and the Isle of Wight and to a smaller extent in Sussex and Surrey, but many have been ploughed out during the last few decades. They generally occur as nucleated groups as in *Greenwich Park* and on *Breach Down* in Kent (figure 39, which shows the group before being encroached upon by a housing estate). On *Farthing Down* (Greater London) they form a linear group

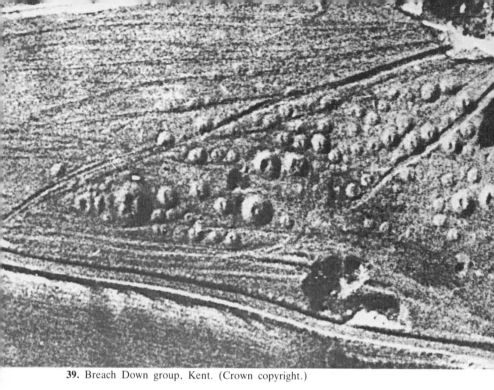

**39.** Breach Down group, Kent. (Crown copyright.)

**40.** Taplow barrow, Buckinghamshire. (Photograph: L. V. Grinsell.)

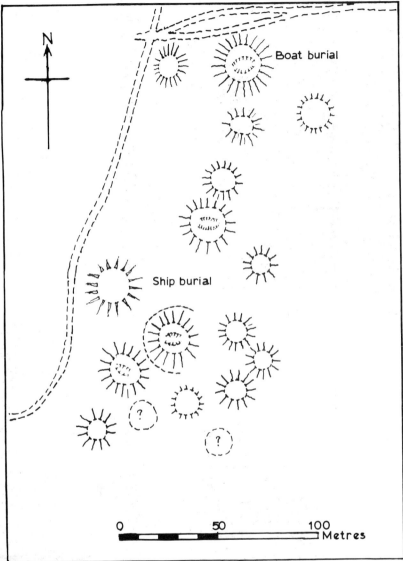

**41.** Sutton Hoo group, Suffolk. The oval depressions in four of the barrows may have resulted from the collapse of wooden boat-burials. (Based on plan by R. L. S. Bruce-Mitford.)

conforming to the long narrow hill on which they are sited. They
are usually 4-8 metres in diameter and up to 1 metre high. The
best surviving groups are those just mentioned and on *Bowcombe
Down* (Isle of Wight). They are believed to date between the mid
sixth and the late seventh centuries.

Saxon intrusive interments were inserted into earlier barrows
both long and round from about AD 550 onwards, especially in
Wiltshire, on the Cotswolds, in the Peak District and on the
Yorkshire Wolds (where more correctly known as Anglian).

**Viking barrows**

In the area covered by this book Viking barrows are known
only in the Midlands and the north of England. They are more
frequent in Ireland, Scotland and the Isle of Man. A small cairn
at *Hesket in the Forest*, Cumbria, removed in 1822, covered an
interment with sword and other warrior trappings. A round
barrow at *Aspatria* in the same county, opened in 1789, contained
a male inhumation with sword, dagger, remains of shield, axe and
gold brooch in a stone-lined grave with decorated wall-slabs. A
group of about 62 small cairns in Heath Wood, *Ingleby*, yielded
cremations with warrior equipment. Occasionally a bronze age
barrow was used for an intrusive Viking interment, as with a
barrow at *Claughton Hall* (Lancashire).

# 9
# Museums

Only the more important items held are stated. Intending visitors are advised to find out the times of opening before making a special journey.

*Alnwick Castle Museum of Antiquities*, Alnwick Castle, Alnwick, Northumberland NE66 1NQ. Telephone: 0665 510777. Much material from barrows in Sussex as well as Northumbria.

*Ashmolean Museum of Art and Archaeology*, Beaumont Street, Oxford OX1 2PH. Telephone: 0865 278000. Finds from Barrow Hills (Radley) and many other sites.

*Bourne Hall Museum*, Spring Street, Ewell, Epsom, Surrey KT17 1UF. Telephone: 01-393 9573. Warrior burial from Saxon grave-mound at Banstead.

*Brighton Art Gallery and Museum*, Church Street, Brighton, East Sussex BN1 1UE. Telephone: 0273 603005. Grave-group with amber cup from the Hove barrow.

*The British Museum*, Great Russell Street, London WC1B 3DG. Telephone: 01-636 1555. The J. C. Atkinson collection from Cleveland; the Durden collection from Dorset; the Greenwell collection from the northern counties; the Jewitt collection from Derbyshire; the Martin Atkins collection from the Lambourn Seven Barrows; the gold cape from Mold (Clwyd); the gold cup from the Rillaton barrow; material from the Sutton Hoo and Taplow barrows.

*Cambridge University Museum of Archaeology and Anthropology*, Downing Street, Cambridge CB2 3DZ. Telephone: 0223 337733 or 333516. Finds from barrows at Bincombe (Dorset), Landford (New Forest) and the Therfield Heath long barrow (Hertfordshire).

*Carlisle Museum and Art Gallery*, Tullie House, Castle Street, Carlisle, Cumbria CA3 8TP. Telephone: 0228 34781. Grave-group from Viking barrow at Hesket in the Forest.

*Castle Museum*, Norwich, Norfolk NR1 3JU. Telephone: 0603 611277 extension 7224. The Little Cressingham grave-group and other finds from Norfolk barrows.

*City of Bristol Museum and Art Gallery*, Queens Road, Bristol, Avon BS8 1RL. Telephone: 0272 299771. Finds from Mendip barrows opened by Skinner; Pool Farm foot-carved cist-slab; urns from the Deverel barrow.

*Colchester and Essex Museum*, The Castle, Colchester, Essex
  CO1 1TJ. Telephone: 0206 712490. Finds from the Lexden
  iron age barrow and the Mersea Mount Roman barrow.
*Corinium Museum*, Park Street, Cirencester, Gloucestershire
  GL7 2BX. Telephone: 0285 5611. Finds and reconstructed
  burial chamber from the Hazleton North long barrow.
*Cornwall County Museum*, (Royal Institution of Cornwall), 25
  River Street, Truro, Cornwall TR1 2SJ. Telephone: 0872
  72205. The main museum for the Cornish material.
*Devizes Museum* (Wiltshire Archaeological and Natural History
  Society), 41 Long Street, Devizes, Wiltshire SN10 1NS. Tele-
  phone: 0380 77369. The Cunnington/Colt Hoare collection;
  finds from the West Kennet long barrow and the Snail Down
  group.
*Dorset County Museum*, High West Street, Dorchester, Dorset
  DT1 1XA. Telephone: 0305 62735. Finds from excavations by
  Charles Warne, Edward Cunnington and later archaeologists.
*Gloucester City Museum and Art Gallery*, Brunswick Road,
  Gloucester GL1 1HP. Telephone: 0452 24131. Material from
  long and round barrows on the Cotswolds.
*Hull and East Riding Museum*, 36 High Street, Hull, North
  Humberside HU1 1NQ. Telephone: 0482 222737 or 222738.
  The J. R. Mortimer collection.
*Ipswich Museum*, High Street, Ipswich, Suffolk IP1 3QH. Tele-
  phone: 0473 213761 or 213762. Material from local barrows.
*Liverpool Museum*, William Brown Street, Liverpool, Mersey-
  side L3 8EN. Telephone: 051-207 0001 or 5451. The Bryan
  Faussett collection of finds from Saxon grave-mounds in Kent.
*Luton Museum and Art Gallery*, Wardown Park, Luton, Bedford-
  shire LU2 7HA. Telephone: 0582 36941 or 36942. Finds from
  the Five Knolls near Dunstable.
*Maidstone Museum and Art Gallery*, St Faith's Street, Maidstone,
  Kent ME14 1LH. Telephone: 0622 54497. Finds from long and
  round barrows in Kent.
*Museum of Antiquities of the University and the Society of
  Antiquaries of Newcastle upon Tyne*, The University, Newcastle
  upon Tyne, Tyne and Wear NE1 7RU. Telephone: 091-222
  6000 extension 6844 or 6849. Gold ornaments from barrows at
  Alston and Redesdale.
*Museum of Sussex Archaeology*, Barbican House, 169 High
  Street, Lewes, East Sussex BN7 1YE. Telephone: 0273 474379.
  Finds from barrows on the Sussex downs.

*Museum of Welsh Antiquities*, Ffordd Gwynedd, Bangor, Gwynedd LL57 1DT. Telephone: 0248 353368. Finds from barrows in North Wales.

*National Museum of Wales*, Cathays Park, Cardiff, South Glamorgan CF1 3NP. Telephone: 0222 397951. The main collection of finds from barrows in Wales.

*Plymouth City Museum and Art Gallery*, Drake Circus, Plymouth, Devon PL4 8AJ. Telephone: 0752 668000 extension 4878. Material from cairns on Dartmoor including the stone cist from Langstone Moor.

*Rotunda Museum of Archaeology and Local History*, Museum Terrace, Vernon Road, Scarborough, North Yorkshire YO11 2HB. Telephone: 0723 374839. The tree-trunk coffin and grave-group from Gristhorpe.

*Royal Albert Memorial Museum*, Queen Street, Exeter, Devon EX4 3RX. Telephone: 0392 265858. Finds from barrows at Upton Pyne and the Broad Down area.

*Salisbury and South Wiltshire Museum*, The King's House, 65 The Close, Salisbury, Wiltshire SP1 2EN. Telephone: 0722 332151. Finds from barrows on Salisbury Plain and in the New Forest.

*Sheffield City Museum*, Weston Park, Sheffield, South Yorkshire S10 2TP. Telephone: 0742 768588. The Bateman collection from barrows in Derbyshire and Staffordshire; the Heathcote collection from barrows on Stanton Moor.

*Somerset County Museum*, Taunton Castle, Castle Green, Taunton, Somerset TA1 4AA. Telephone: 0823 255504. Finds from Wick Barrow and other sites.

*Winchester City Museum*, The Square, Winchester, Hampshire SO23 9ES. Telephone: 0962 848269. Objects from long and round barrows in Hampshire.

*Yorkshire Museum*, Museum Gardens, York, North Yorkshire YO1 2DR. Telephone: 0904 629745. Finds from iron age square barrows at Arras and the Danes' Graves.

# 10
# Further reading

(Works quoted in full in the text are not here repeated.)

**History of study**

Cunnington, R. H. (editor James Dyer). *From Antiquary to Archaeologist: a Biography of William Cunnington 1754-1810*. Shire Publications, 1975.

Jessup, R. F. *Man of Many Talents: An Informal Biography of James Douglas 1753-1819*. Phillimore, 1975.

Lester, G. A. 'Thomas Bateman, Barrow Digger', *Derbyshire Archaeological Journal*, 93 (1973), 10-22.

Roese, H. E. 'The Victorian Barrow-diggers of Wales', *Bulletin of the Board of Celtic Studies*, 33 (1986), 236-44; 34 (1987), 205-19.

Woodbridge, Kenneth. *Landscape and Antiquity*. Oxford University Press, 1970. Part iii (187-234) deals with the barrow diggings of Hoare and Cunnington.


**General**

Grinsell, L. V. *The Ancient Burial-Mounds of England*. Methuen, second edition 1953; reprint, Greenwood Press, Westport, Connecticut, 1975. Reprint has introduction and bibliography to 1973.


**Neolithic**

Ashbee, P. *The Earthen Long Barrow in Britain*. Dent, second edition 1984.

Atkinson, R. J. C. 'Wayland's Smithy', *Antiquity*, 39 (1965), 126-33.

Britnell, W. J., and Savory, H. N. *Gwernvale and Penywyrlod: Two Neolithic Long Cairns in the Black Mountains of Brecknock*. Cardiff, 1984.

Corcoran, J. X. W. P. 'The Cotswold-Severn Group' in T. G. E. Powell (editor), *Megalithic Enquiries*, 13-106. Liverpool University Press, 1969.

Corcoran, J. X. W. P. 'Multi-period Construction and the Origins of the Chambered Long Cairn ...', in F. Lynch and C. Burgess (editors), *Prehistoric Man in Wales and the West*, 31-63. Adams and Dart, Bath, 1972.

Darvill, T. C. *The Megalithic Chambered Tombs of the Cotswold-Severn Region*. Vorda Publications, 25 Bute Close, Highworth, Wiltshire, 1982.

Kinnes, I. *Round Barrows and Ring Ditches in the British Neolithic*. British Museum Occasional Papers, 7, 1979.

Lynch, Frances. 'The Megalithic Tombs of North Wales' in T. G. E. Powell (editor), *Megalithic Enquiries*, 107-74. Liverpool University Press, 1969.

Manby, T. G. 'Chambered Tombs of Derbyshire', *Derbyshire Archaeological Journal*, 78 (1958), 25-39.

Manby, T. G. 'Long Barrows in Northern England', *Scottish Archaeological Forum*, 2 (1970), 1-27.

Masters, L. 'The Neolithic Long Cairns of Cumbria and Northumberland' in R. Miket and C. Burgess (editors), *Between and Beyond the Walls: Essays in Honour of George Jobey*, 52-73. John Donald, Edinburgh, 1984.

Piggott, S. *The West Kennet Long Barrow*. HMSO, 1962.

Royal Commission on Historical Monuments. *Long Barrows in Hampshire and the Isle of Wight*, 1979.

Saville, A., and Selkirk, A. 'Hazleton', *Current Archaeology*, VIII (4) (1983), 107-12.
Thomas, J., and Whittle, A. 'Anatomy of a Tomb: West Kennet Revisited', *Oxford Journal of Archaeology*, 5 (1986), 129-56.

**Bronze age**
Ashbee, P. *The Bronze Age Round Barrow in Britain*. Phoenix House, 1960.
Case, H. J. 'The Lambourn Seven Barrows', *Berkshire Archaeological Journal*, 55 (1957), 15-31.
Crawford, G. M. *Bronze Age Burial Mounds in Cleveland*. Cleveland County Council, Middlesbrough, 1980.
Dyer, J. F. 'Barrows of the Chilterns', *Archaeological Journal*, 106 (1959), 1-24.
Fox, Sir Cyril. *Life and Death in the Bronze Age*. Routledge and Kegan Paul, 1959.
Grinsell, L. V. *Archaeology of Wessex*. Methuen, 1958.
Grinsell, L. V. *Dorset Barrows*. Dorset Natural History and Archaeological Society, Dorchester, 1959.
Grinsell, L. V. 'Somerset Barrows', *Somerset Archaeology and Natural History*, 113 and 115 (1970-2), supplements.
Grinsell, L. V. 'Disc-barrows', *Proceedings of the Prehistoric Society*, 40 (1974), 79-112.
Grinsell, L. V. *The Stonehenge Barrow Groups*. Salisbury and South Wiltshire Museum, 1978.
Grinsell, L. V. 'Dartmoor Barrows', *Proceedings of the Devon Archaeological Society*, 36 for 1978 (1979), 85-180.
Grinsell, L. V. *Dorset Barrows Supplement*. Dorset Natural History and Archaeological Society, Dorchester, 1982.
Grinsell, L. V. 'The Barrows of South and East Devon', *Proceedings of the Devon Archaeological Society*, 41 (1983), 5-46.
Grinsell, L. V. 'Surrey Barrows 1934-86: A Reappraisal', *Surrey Archaeological Collections*, 78 (1987), 1-41.
Grinsell, L. V. 'Somerset Barrows: Revisions 1971-87', *Somerset Archaeology and Natural History*, 131 (1988), 13-26.
Grinsell, L. V., and Sherwin, G. A. 'Isle of Wight Barrows', *Proceedings of the Isle of Wight Natural History and Archaeological Society*, 3 (1941), 179-222.
Gunstone, A. J. H. 'Archaeological Gazetteer of Staffordshire. II: The Barrows', *North Staffordshire Journal of Field Studies*, 5 (1965), 20-63.
Lawson, A. J., *et al*. 'The Barrows of East Anglia', *East Anglian Archaeology*, 12 (1981).
Lawson, A. J., *et al*. 'Barrow Excavations in Norfolk 1950-82', *East Anglian Archaeology*, 29 (1986).
Lynch, Frances. 'Ring Cairns ... in Wales', *Scottish Archaeological Forum*, 4 (1972), 61-80.
Marsden, B. M. *The Burial Mounds of Derbyshire*. Privately printed, 1977.
O'Neil, Helen, and Grinsell, L. V. 'Gloucestershire Barrows', *Transactions of the Bristol and Gloucestershire Archaeological Society*, 79 (i) (1960), 1-148.
Petersen, F. 'Early Bronze Age Timber Graves and Coffin Burials on the Yorkshire Wolds', *Yorkshire Archaeological Journal*, 42 (1971), 262-7.
Savory, H. N. 'Cists and Cist-cairns in Wales' in F. Lynch and C. Burgess (editors), *Prehistoric Man in Wales and the West*, 107-16. Adams and Dart, Bath, 1972.
Trahair, J. 'A Survey of Cairns on Bodmin Moor', *Cornish Archaeology*, 17 (1978), 3-24.

Young, R. 'An Inventory of Barrows in County Durham', *Transactions of the Architectural and Archaeological Society of Durham and Northumberland*, NS 5 (1980), 1-16.

**Iron age**

Foster, Jennifer. *The Lexden Tumulus*. British Archaeological Reports, British series, 156, 1986.
Stead, Ian. *The Arras Culture*. Yorkshire Philosophical Society, York, 1979.
White, D. A. 'Iron Age ... Barrow near Handley, Dorset', *Antiquaries' Journal*, 50 (1970), 26-36.

**Roman**

Charlton, B. *et al*. 'The Roman Cemetery at Petty Knowes, Rochester, Northumberland', *Archaeologia Aeliana*, 5, series xii (1984), 1-31.
Fowler, P. J. 'A Roman Barrow at Knob's Crook, Woodlands, Dorset', *Antiquaries' Journal*, 45 (1965), 22-51.
Jessup, R. F. 'Barrows and Walled Cemeteries in Roman Britain', *Journal of the British Archaeological Association*, NS 22 (1959), 1-32.
Wilson, R. J. A. *Roman Remains in Britain*. Constable, third edition 1988.

**Anglo-Saxon**

Arnold, C. J. *The Anglo-Saxon Cemeteries of the Isle of Wight*. British Museum, 1982.
Bruce-Mitford, R. L. S. *The Sutton Hoo Ship Burial: a Handbook*. British Museum, 1979.
Meaney, Audrey. *Gazetteer of Early Anglo-Saxon Burial Sites*. George Allen and Unwin, 1964.

**Viking**

Cowen, J. D. 'Viking Burials in Cumbria', *Transactions of the Cumberland and Westmorland Antiquarian and Archaeological Society*, NS 48 (1948), 73-6; 67 (1967), 31-4.

# Site index

The information is given in the following order: site, county, national grid reference, period, page number. Numbers in italic refer to illustrations.

Adam's Grave, Wiltshire. SU 112634. Neolithic. 11
Addington, Kent. TQ 653592. Neolithic. 20
Advent, Cornwall. SX 137834. Bronze age. 30
Amesbury Down, Wiltshire. SU 148394. Bronze age. 30
Anmer, Norfolk. TF 755289. Bronze age. 44
Arras, Humberside. SE 930413. Iron age. 49
Arthur's Stone, Glamorgan. SS 491905. Neolithic. 25
Ashen Hill, Somerset. ST 539521. Bronze age. 33
Aspatria, Cumbria. NY 142419. Viking. 56
Asthall, Oxfordshire. SP 289101. Saxon. 53
Avening, Gloucestershire. ST 879984. Neolithic. 13, 15
Bant's Carn, Scilly. SV 911124. Neolithic. 27
Barclodiad y Gawres, Gwynedd. SH 329707. Neolithic. 24
Bartlow Hills, Essex. TL 586448. Roman. 51, 51
Beacon Batch, Somerset. ST 485571. Bronze age. 33
Belas Knap, Gloucestershire. SP 021254. Neolithic. 13, 14
Benty Grange, Derbyshire. SK 146642. Saxon. 53
Bircham Common, Norfolk. TF 775316. Bronze age. 44
Blawearie, Northumberland. NU 082223. Bronze age. 45
Bowcombe Down, Isle of Wight. SZ 461874. Saxon. 56
Bow Hill, West Sussex. SU 820111. Bronze age. 42
Brane, Cornwall. SW 401282. Neolithic. 26, 27
Breach Down, Kent. TR 207490. Saxon. 53, 54
Brenig, Clwyd. SH 984575. Bronze age. 42
Bridestones, Cheshire. SJ 906622. Neolithic. 23, 24
Broad Down, Devon. SY 175945. Bronze age. 32
Bryn Celli Ddu, Gwynedd. SH 508702. Neolithic. 24, 25
Bryn yr Ellyllon, Clwyd. SJ 247638. Bronze age. 47, 48, 48
Bryn yr Hen Bobl, Gwynedd. SH 519690. Neolithic. 24
Bush Barrow, Wiltshire. SU 116412. Bronze age. 5, 38
Carland Cross, Cornwall. SW 847540. Bronze age. 30
Carn Bugail, Glamorgan. SO 100035. Bronze age. 43
Cefn Bryn, Glamorgan. SS 490905. Bronze age. 43
Centre Hill, North Yorkshire. SE 288791. Bronze age. 44
Chapman Barrows, Devon. SS 695435. Bronze age. 33
Chestnuts, Kent. TQ 652592. Neolithic. 23
Clandon Barrow, Dorset. SY 656890. Bronze age. 42
Claughton Hall, Lancashire. SD 524424. Viking. 56

Coldrum, Kent. TQ 654607. Neolithic. 20, 22
Corringdon Ball, Devon. SX 670614. Neolithic. 24
Crooksbury Hill, Surrey. SU 894450. Bronze age. 30
Crug yr Afan, Glamorgan. SS 920954. Bronze age. 43
Culliford Tree, Dorset. SY 703853. Neolithic. 42
Danby Rigg, North Yorkshire. NZ 710065. Uncertain. 4
Dane John Mound, Kent. TR 148574. Roman. 52
Danes' Hills, Skipwith Common, Humberside. SE 645377. Iron age. 49
Deverel Barrow, Dorset. SY 820990. Bronze age. 47
Devil's Humps, West Sussex. SU 820111. Bronze age. 42
Devil's Jumps, West Sussex. SU 825173. Bronze age. 42
Duggleby Howe, North Yorkshire. SE 880669. Neolithic. 9, 10
East Heslerton, North Yorkshire. SE 939753. Neolithic. 11
East Kennet, Wiltshire. SU 116699. Neolithic. 19
Eastlow Hill, Suffolk. TL 900617. Roman. 51
Farthing Down, Greater London. TQ 300580. Saxon. 53
Farway, Devon. SY 162951. Bronze age. 32
Fernworthy, Devon. SX 667843. Bronze age. 31, 32
Five Barrows, Devon. SS 732368. Bronze age. 33
Five Barrows, Northumberland. NT 953020. Bronze age. 46
Five Knolls, Bedfordshire. TL 007210. Bronze age. 30, 43
Five Wells, Derbyshire. SK 124711. Neolithic. 27, 28
Flat Howe, North Yorkshire. NZ 855046. Bronze age. 45, 45
Foel Trigarn, Dyfed. SN 158336. Bronze age. 42
Fussell's Lodge, Wiltshire. SU 192324. Neolithic. 12
Garleigh Moor, Northumberland. NZ 052992. Bronze age 45, 46
Garton Slack, Humberside. SE 930413. Iron age. 49
Gelligaer Common group, Glamorgan. SO 100035. Bronze age. 43
Gib Hill, Derbyshire. SK 159633. Neolithic/bronze age. 44
Gittisham Hill, Devon. SY 149968. Bronze age. 32
Great Carn, Glamorgan. SS 491907. Bronze age. 43
Green Low, Derbyshire. SK 233580. Neolithic. 29
Greenwich Park group, Greater London. TQ 388771. Saxon. 53
Grey Mare and Colts, Dorset. SY 584871. Neolithic. 24

Hamel Down group, Devon. SX 706793. Bronze age. 32

Handley, Dorset. ST 989144. Iron age. 49

Harpley Common, Norfolk. TF 765280. Bronze age. 44

Hazleton North, Gloucestershire. SP 073189. Neolithic. 8, 58

Hepburn Moor, Northumberland. NU 082231. Bronze age. 45

Hesket in the Forest, Cumbria. NY 469455. Viking. 56

Heston Brake, Gwent. ST 506887. Neolithic. 20

Hetty Pegler's Tump, Gloucestershire. SO 790000. Neolithic. 17

Ingleby, Derbyshire. SK 343257. Viking. 56

Julliberrie's Grave, Kent. TQ 077532. Neolithic. 20

Kit's Coty, Kent. TQ 745608. Neolithic. 20, 22

Knob's Crook, Dorset. SU 052073. Roman. 51

Knowlton, Dorset. SU 026103. Bronze age. 35

Lakehead Hill, Devon. SX 645776. Bronze age. 31

Lambourn Seven Barrows, Berkshire. SU 328828. Bronze age. 38-9, 39

Lanyon, Cornwall. SW 430337. Neolithic. 24

Lexden, Essex. TL 975247. Iron age. 49

Little Cressingham, Norfolk. TL 861990. Bronze age. 43

Llanmadoc Hill, Glamorgan. SS 430927. Bronze age. 43

Long Bredy, Dorset. SY 572911. Neolithic. 11, 11, 42

Loose Howe, North Yorkshire. NZ 703008. Bronze age. 44

Lower Kit's Coty, Kent. TQ 745604. Neolithic. 20

Lowther, Cumbria, NY 537243. Neolithic. 11.

Maiden Castle bank-barrow, Dorset. SY 668885. Neolithic. 11

Mersea Mount, Essex. TM 023143. Roman. 52

Minninglow, Derbyshire. SK 209573. Neolithic. 27

Nine-barrow Down, Dorset. SY 995816. Bronze age. 5, 42

Normanton Down, Wiltshire (mortuary enclosure). SU 114410. Neolithic. 12

Normanton group, Wiltshire. SU 120413. Bronze age. 38

Notgrove, Gloucestershire. SP 096212. Neolithic. 9

Nympsfield, Gloucestershire. SO 794013. Neolithic. 9, 17

Oakley Down group, Dorset. SU 018173. Bronze age. 39, 40-1

Old Down Field, Somerset. ST 659427. Bronze age. 33

Overton Hill, Wiltshire. SU 120682. Roman. 51

Parc Cwm, Glamorgan. SS 537899. Neolithic. 19

Pelynt group, Cornwall. SW 200545. Bronze age. 30

Pen-y-Wyrlod, Powys. SO 225398. Neolithic. 9

Petty Knowes, Northumberland. NY 835983. Roman. 51

Pimperne, Dorset. ST 917105. Neolithic. 12

Plas Newydd, Anglesey, Gwynedd. SH 520697. Neolithic. 25

Pool Farm, Mendip, Somerset. ST 537541. Bronze age. 33

Priddy Nine Barrows, Somerset. ST 538515.

Bronze age. 33

Rhossili Down, Glamorgan. SS 421890. Bronze age. 42

Rillaton, Cornwall. SX 260719. Bronze age. 30, 31

Rodmarton, Gloucestershire. ST 932973. Neolithic. 14

St Lythans, Glamorgan. ST 101723. Neolithic. 15

Sales Lot, Withington, Gloucestershire. SP 049157. Neolithic. 9

Scorborough group, Humberside. TA 017453. Iron age. 49

Scutchamer Knob, Oxfordshire. SU 457850. Saxon (?). 53

Setta Barrow, Devon. SS 726381. Bronze age. 33

Seven Hills, Norfolk. TL 904814, Bronze age. 43

Silbury Hill, Wiltshire. SU 100685. Neolithic. 9, 10

Six Hills, Hertfordshire. TL 237237. Roman. 51

Soldiers' Grave, Gloucestershire. SO 794015. Neolithic (?). 9

Stanton Moor group, Derbyshire. SK 249633 (centre). Bronze age. 44

Stoney Littleton, Avon. ST 735572. Neolithic. 17, 19, 20-1

Sutton Hoo group, Suffolk. TM 287487 (centre). Saxon. 53, 55

Sweyne's Howes, Glamorgan. SS 421898. Neolithic. 25

Taphouse ridge group, Cornwall. SX 140633 (centre). Bronze age. 30

Taplow, Buckinghamshire. SU 906821. Saxon. 53, 54

Therfield Heath group, Hertfordshire. TL 342403. Neolithic/bronze age. 11, 12, 43

Thornborough, Buckinghamshire. SP 732333. Roman. 51, 52

Three Barrows, Devon. SX 653626. Bronze age. 32

Tinkinswood, Glamorgan. ST 092733. Neolithic. 14-15, 15

Two Barrows (Dartmoor), Devon. SX 706793. Bronze age. 32

Two Barrows (Exmoor), Devon. SX 747363. Bronze age. 33

Ty Illtud, Powys. SO 098264. Neolithic. 17

Ty Isaf, Powys. SO 182291. Neolithic. 15

Upwey, Dorset. SY 663866. Bronze age. 35, 35

Veryan Beacon, Cornwall. SX 913387. Bronze age. 30

Wayland's Smithy, Oxfordshire. SU 281854. Neolithic. 9, 11, 16-17

Weasenham Lyngs group, Norfolk. TF 853198. Bronze age. 43

West Kennet, Wiltshire. SU 104677. Neolithic. 18, 19

Willy Howe, Humberside. TA 063724. Neolithic. 9

Windmill Tump, Gloucestershire. ST 932973. Neolithic. 14

Winterbourne Stoke Crossroads group, Wiltshire. SU 401417 (centre). Neolithic and bronze age. 12, 36-7, 38

Winterslow, Wiltshire. SU 228354. Bronze age. 34, 35

Wor Barrow, Dorset. SU 012173. Neolithic. 12.